CW00725376

Love *n* 1. warm affection *v* 2. to have strong or deep tender feelings for

Love… grows into the soul,
Warms every vein, and beats in
every pulse…

Joseph Addison (1672-1719)

Our love is like the misty rain that
falls softly, but floods the river.

African proverb

Love is a great beautifier.

Louisa May Alcott (1832-1888)

In melody divine,
My heart it beats to rapturous love,
I long to call you mine.

Author Unknown

A hundred hearts would be too few
To carry all my love for you.

Author Unknown

Love is the only gold.

Alfred, Lord Tennyson (1809-1883)

Life is a flower of which
love is the honey.

Victor Hugo (1802-1885)

In spite of myself, my imagination carries me to you. I grasp you, I kiss you, I caress you, a thousand of the most amorous caresses take possession of me.

Honoré de Balzac (1799-1850), in a letter to Evelina Hanska, June 1836

…it is impossible to love, and to be wise.

Francis Bacon (1561-1626), from "Of Love"

The consciousness of loving and being loved brings a warmth and richness to life that nothing else can bring.

Oscar Wilde (1854-1900)

All love that has not friendship for its base, is like a mansion built upon the sand.

Ella Wheeler Wilcox (1850-1919)

He felt now that he was not simply close to her, but that he did not know where he ended and she began.

Leo Tolstoy (1828-1910), from Anna Karenina

We loved with a love that was more than love.

Edgar Allan Poe (1809-1849)

But true love is a durable fire,
In the mind ever burning,
Never sick, never old, never dead,
From itself never turning.

Sir Walter Raleigh (1552-1618)

There is only one happiness in life,
to love and be loved.

*George Sand (Amandine Aurore Lucie
Dupin) (1804-1876)*

Love holds me captive again
and I tremble with bittersweet
longing.

Sappho (c.610-c.580 BC), from "Two Fragments"

Did my heart love till now?
Forswear it sight!
For I ne'er saw true beauty till this
night.

William Shakespeare (1564-1616), from Romeo and Juliet

Shall I compare thee to
a summer's day?
Thou art more lovely
and more temperate…

*William Shakespeare (1564-1616),
from Sonnet XVIII*

...the sunlight clasps the earth,
And the moonbeams kiss the sea —
What are all these kissings worth,
If thou kiss not me?

Percy Bysshe Shelley (1792-1822), from "Love's Philosophy"

Love is the master key that opens the gates of happiness.

Oliver Wendell Holmes (1809-1894)

The most precious possession that ever comes to a man in this world is a woman's heart.

Josiah Gilbert Holland (1819-1881)

Love is the May-day of the heart.

Benjamin Disraeli (1804-1881)

…the heart that has truly loved never forgets.

Thomas Moore (1779-1852)

Soul meets soul on lovers' lips.

Percy Bysshe Shelley (1792-1822)

Love is the emblem of eternity; it confounds all notion of time; effaces all memory of a beginning, all fear of an end.

Madame De Stael (1766-1817)

Two souls, one heart.

French saying

I love thee like puddings; if thou wert pie I'd eat thee.

John Ray (1627-1705)

…you have bereft me of words, Only my blood speaks to you in my veins.

William Shakespeare (1564-1616), from The Merchant of Venice

My lips moved towards hers. We kissed each other. ...It seemed to me that all my life had been narrowed to one perfect moment of rose-coloured joy.

Oscar Wilde (1854-1900), from The Picture of Dorian Gray

I cannot breathe without you.

John Keats (1795-1821), in a letter to Fanny Brawne

You are always new,
The last of your kisses was ever the
sweetest.

John Keats (1795-1821)

I love thee – I love thee!
'Tis all that I can say;
It is my vision in the night,
My dreaming in the day…

*Thomas Hood (1799-1845), from
"I Love Thee"*

Men always want to be a woman's first love…

Oscar Wilde (1854-1900)

I wish I had the gift of making rhymes, for methinks there is poetry in my head and heart since I have been in love with you.

Nathaniel Hawthorne (1804-1864), in a letter to his wife, Sophia

All the sweets of living are for those that love.

The Rubaiyat of Omar Khayyam (c.1048-c.1122)

Who travels for love finds a thousand miles not longer than one.

Japanese proverb

Drink to me only with thine eyes,
And I will pledge with mine;
Or leave a kiss but in the cup
And I'll not look for wine.

*Ben Jonson (1572-1637), from
"To Celia"*

So dear I love him, that with him all deaths I could endure, without him live no life.

John Milton (1608-1674), from Paradise Lost

…you and you alone make me feel that I am alive…. Other men, it is said, have seen angels, but I have seen thee and thou art enough.

George Moore (1852-1933)

Who would give a law to lovers?
Love is unto itself a higher law.

*Boethius, Anicius Manlius Severinus
(c.475–524), from "The Consolation of
Philosophy"*

I love thee to the depth and breadth
and height
My soul can reach....

*Elizabeth Barrett Browning
(1806-1861)*

And you will always be with me.
I shall never cease to be filled with
newness,
Having you near me.

D.H. Lawrence (1885-1930),
from "Wedlock"

Brightest truth, purest trust in the universe, – all were for me
In the kiss of one girl.

Robert Browning (1812-1889), from "Summum Bonum"

How did it happen that their lips came together? How does it happen that birds sing, that snow melts, that the rose unfolds...? A kiss ...

Victor Hugo (1802-1885)

Until then, mio dolce amor, a thousand kisses; but give me none in return, for they set my blood on fire.

Napoleon Bonaparte (1769-1821), in a letter to his wife, Josephine, December 1795

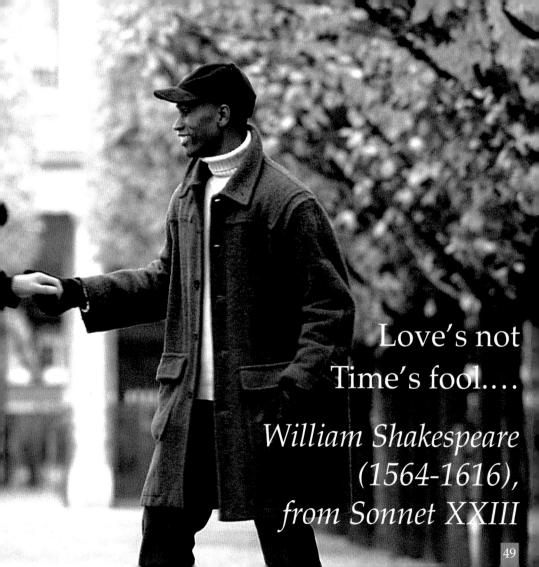

Love's not
Time's fool....

*William Shakespeare
(1564-1616),
from Sonnet XXIII*

Love is the flower of life, and blossoms unexpectedly and without law....

D.H. Lawrence (1885-1930)

There is nothing holier, in this life of ours, than the first consciousness of love – the first fluttering of its silken wings.

Henry Wadsworth Longfellow (1807-1882)

God is Love – I dare say.
But what a mischievous devil Love
is!

Samuel Butler (1612-1680)

She walks in beauty, like the night
Of cloudless climes and starry skies,
And all that's best of dark and
bright
Meets in her aspect and her eyes…

Lord Byron (1788-1824)

I love you not only for what you are,
but for what I am when I am with
you.

*Elizabeth Barrett Browning
(1806-1861)*

O Love, O fire! once he drew
With one long kiss my whole soul
through
My lips, as sunlight drinketh dew.

*Alfred, Lord Tennyson (1809-1892),
from "Fatima"*

You were made perfectly to be loved
and surely I have loved you, in the
idea of you, my whole life long.

Elizabeth Barrett Browning
(1806-1861)

O lyric Love, half-angel and
half-bird
And all a wonder and a wild desire.

Robert Browning (1812-1889)

Whatever our souls are made of, his and mine are the same…

Emily Brontë (1818-1848), from Wuthering Heights

Come live in my heart and pay no rent.

Samuel Lover (1797-1868)

Who, being loved, is poor?

Oscar Wilde (1854-1900)

Come live with me and be my Love,
And we will all the pleasures prove
That hills and valleys, dale and field,
And all the craggy mountains yield.

Christopher Marlowe (1564-1593), from
"The Passionate Shepherd to His Love"

Brightest truth, purest trust in the universe, – all were for me
In the kiss of one girl.

Robert Browning (1812-1889), from "Summum Bonum"

We are all born for love. It is the principle of existence, and its only end.

Benjamin Disraeli (1804-1881), from "Sybil"

Remember tonight, for it is the beginning of always.

Dante Alighieri (1265-1321)

Wild nights! Wild nights!
Were I with thee,
Wild nights should be
Our luxury!

Emily Dickinson (1830–1886), from "Wild Nights"

There is no remedy for love than to love more.

Henry David Thoreau (1817-1862)

Love is the irresistible desire to be irresistibly desired.

Mark Twain (1835-1910)

To live without loving is to not really live.

Molière (1622-1673)

Pillow'd upon my fair Love's ripening breast, To feel for ever its soft fall and swell, Awake for ever in a sweet unrest....

John Keats (1795-1821)

The quarrels of lovers are like summer storms. Everything is more beautiful when they have passed.

Suzanne Curchod Necker (1739-1794)

As fair art thou, my bonnie lass,
So deep in luve am I;
And I will luve thee still, my dear,
Till a' the seas gang dry

Robert Burns (1759-1796)

The simple lack of her is more to me than others' presence.

Edward Thomas (1878-1917), from "Unknown"

…if, when you hold me, and I don't speak, it's because all the words in me seem to have become throbbing pulses…

Edith Wharton (1862-1937), to W. Morton Fullerton

...I love thee with the breath,
Smiles, tears, of all my life....

*Elizabeth Barrett Browning
(1806-1861)*

...ever has it been that love knows
not its own depth until the hour of
separation.

Khalil Gibran (1883-1931)

…you can't come into the room without my feeling all over me a ripple of flame…

Edith Wharton (1862-1937), to W. Morton Fullerton

Love is the joy of the good, the wonder of the wise, the amazement of the Gods.

Plato (c.428-c.348 BC)

Love, in courtship, is friendship in hope; in matrimony, friendship upon proof.

Samuel Richardson (1689-1761), in a letter to Hester Mulso

I would eat of thy flesh as of
delicate fruit,
I am drunk of its smell, and the
scent of thy tresses
Is a flame that devours.

George Moore (1852-1933)

…love… makes one little room, an
everywhere.

*John Donne (1572-1631), from
"The Good Morrow"*

Nothing in the world is single,
All things by a law divine
In one another's being mingle –
Why not I with thine?

*Percy Bysshe Shelley
(1792-1822)*

Marrying for love may be a bit risky, but it is so honest that God can't help but smile on it.

Josh Billings (1818-1885)

If thou must love me, let it be for naught except for love's sake only.

Elizabeth Barrett Browning (1806-1861)

I almost wish we were butterflies and lived but three summer days – three such days with you I could fill with more delight than fifty common years could ever contain.

John Keats (1795-1821), in a letter to Fanny Brawne, July 1819

At the touch of love, everyone becomes a poet.

Plato (c.428-348 BC)

The magic of first love is our ignorance that it can ever end.

Benjamin Disraeli (1804-1881)

The most powerful symptom of love is a tenderness which becomes at times almost insupportable.

Victor Hugo (1802-1885)

Love is the answer.

Author Unknown

…to get the full value of a joy you must have somebody to divide it with.

Mark Twain (1835-1910)

Familiar acts are beautiful through love.

Percy Bysshe Shelley (1792-1822)

One word frees us of all the weight and pain of life, that word is love.

Sophocles (c.496-c.405 BC)

Many are the stars I see, but in my eye no star like thee.

English saying

Love is life. All, everything that I understand, I understand only because I love.

Leo Tolstoy (1828-1910)

'Tis better to have loved and lost than never to have loved at all.

Alfred, Lord Tennyson (1809-1883)

This edition published in 2008 by Bizzybee Publishing Ltd. Text by Claire Fletcher.
© bizzybee publishing 2008 Printed in China